My Feelings

ANGER

Published by Creative Education
123 South Broad Street
Mankato, Minnesota 56001

Creative Education is an imprint of
THE CREATIVE COMPANY.

Design and production by EVANSDAY DESIGN

My Feelings

NGER

LENORE FRANZEN

LIBRARY OF CONGRESS CATALOGING-IN-PUBLICATION DATA

Franzen, Lenore.
Anger / by Lenore Franzen.
p. cm. — (My feelings)
Includes bibliographical references and index.
ISBN 1-58341-318-9
1. Anger—Juvenile literature. I. Title.

BF575.A5F7 2004
152.4'7—dc22   2004049338

First Edition
9 8 7 6 5 4 3 2 1

PHOTOGRAPHS BY: Corbis (Siggi Bucher/NewSport, Dex Images, Duomo, Bob Krist,
Brad Mangin/NewSport, James Noble, Todd Pearson, Steve Prezant, Reuters,
Royalty-Free, Norbert Schaefer, Mike Segar/Reuters Newmedia Inc., ML Sinibaldi,
Ariel Skelley, LWA-Dann Tardif, Chris Trotman/NewSport, Larry Williams)

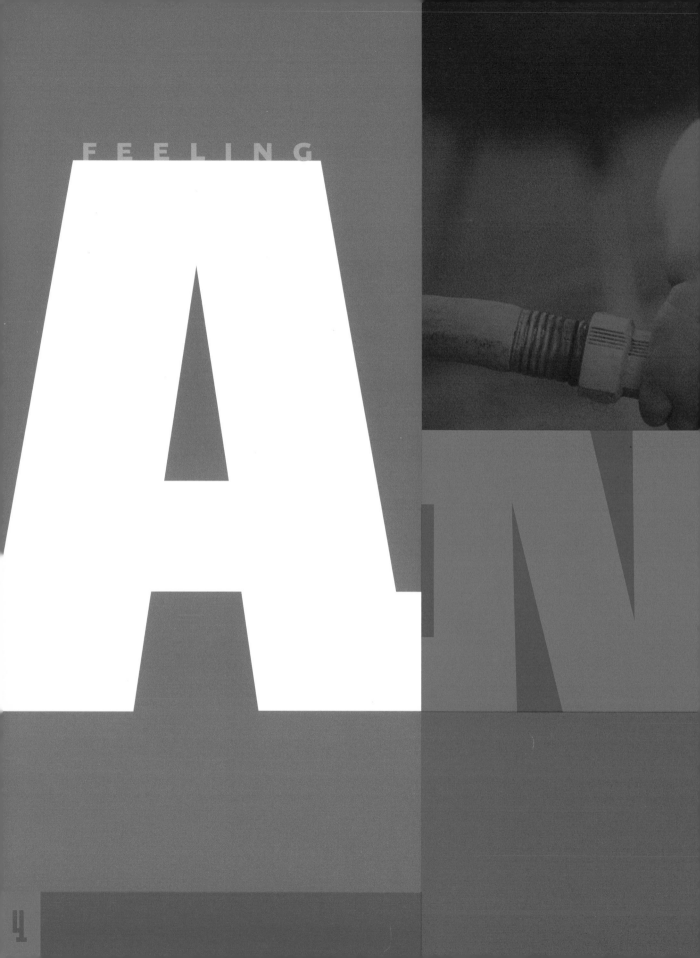

FEELING

A

N

GRY

A normal heart beats about 70 times a minute. Anger makes it beat faster.

People feel many different things. They can feel happy, afraid, sad, or mad. These feelings are called emotions. Anger is an emotion. Another word for *angry* is *mad*.

Everyone feels anger. When you are mad, you may stomp your feet or yell. You may kick or hit something. You do not feel good when you are angry.

When two people are mad at each other, they may fight. When two countries are angry at each other, they may go to war. Too much anger can hurt people.

emot

When you *blow up*, *boil over*, *see red*,
or *hit the ceiling*, you are mad.

WHAT MAKES

Y_{OU}

Think of a time when you were angry. Do you remember what made you mad? Did you get in trouble for something you did not do? Did someone take something of yours? Or call you names?

You may feel angry when someone disappoints you. Maybe your dad is too busy to play with you. Or your friend forgets your birthday. You may get mad when you do not get what you want. Maybe your mom will not buy you ice cream. Maybe you lose a game.

Little things may bother you, too. You may have to eat food you do not like. You may rip your new shirt. Or be too short to reach something. When many little things happen, you may get angry.

Sometimes, a funny face or a joke can help you forget your anger.

points

11

A N

GER

A sudden, violent show of
anger is called a tantrum.

When you are mad, your body shows it. You breathe faster. Your face turns red. Your muscles tighten. Your body feels like it has a lot of energy. It is okay to let your anger out. But only if it does not hurt you or someone else.

You may try not to let your anger show. But keeping your anger inside for a long time is bad. You might get **rashes**, stomachaches, or other health problems. You may not sleep well. Anger can also make it hard to think. You may have a hard time learning in school.

rashe

The smell of some plants, such as lavender, can help people forget their anger.

GOOD-BYE TO

A

N

EMERGENCY DOOR

GER

Seeing the color blue can help angry
people calm down and relax.

You can do many things to get rid of your anger in a healthy way. Try counting to 10. Take deep breaths. Think about a place you really like, such as a park, the zoo, or the beach. Talk about your anger with someone you trust. Ask for help. Draw a picture of how you feel. Write a story. Ride your bike.

Everyone gets mad. And it is okay to be angry once in a while. With practice, you can learn to turn your anger into something good.

trust

19

ANGRY PEOPLE

Does everyone feel anger the same way? Do this activity and find out!

What You Need

THREE KIDS AND THREE GROWN-UPS

PAPER

A PENCIL

What You Do

1. Ask everyone this question: "If your friend broke your favorite toy, what would you do?"

2. Write down the answers.

3. Share the answers with a grown-up. What would the kids do? What would the grown-ups do? Would kids do the same things as grown-ups? What would the grown-ups do that is different? Talk about good ways to make anger go away.

WORDS TO KNOW

disappoints   lets you down; does not do what you were hoping for

emotions   feelings; happiness and sadness are kinds of emotions

muscles   parts of the body that help you move

rashes   reddish marks on your skin

trust   believe or feel safe with

READ MORE
EXPLORE THE WEB

Kroll, Steven. *That Makes Me Mad!* New York: SeaStar Books, 2002.

Lachner, Dorothea. *Andrew's Angry Words*. New York: North-South Books, 1995.

Lichtenheld, Tom. *What Are You So Grumpy About?*
Boston: Little, Brown and Co., 2003.

Thomas, Pat. *Is It Right to Fight?* Hauppauge, N.Y.:
Barron's Educational Series, 2003.

AMERICA'S CHILDREN: BOOKS ABOUT CONFLICT RESOLUTION
http://www.pampetty.com/conflictresolution.htm

KIDSHEALTH: DEALING WITH ANGER
http://www.kidshealth.org/kid/feeling/emotion/anger.html

INDEX